Moments with God

Songs of Praise and Thanksgiving

from the Bible

Frank Dell'Isola

COLLINS

Cleveland · New York

William Collins Publishers, Inc.
Cleveland · New York

Canticles from the Good News Bible-Old Testament: Copyright American
Bible Society 1976: Deuterocanonicals/Apocrypha: Copyright American
Bible Society 1979: New Testament: Copyright American Bible Society
1966, 1971, 1976. Used by permission.

First published 1979

COPYRIGHT © 1979 BY FRANK DELL'ISOLA

Library of Congress Cataloging in Publication Data
Dell'Isola, Frank.
   Moments with God.
   1. Bible—Meditations. I. Title.
BS483.5.D44   220.7'7   79-16705
ISBN 0-529-05668-2

Printed in the United States of America

A Dedication

To my beloved Gretchen, whose Mosaic

way of life made this book possible.

Contents

INTRODUCTORY NOTE

From beginning to end the Bible is rich in poetry, prayer, drama, and politics, through all of which the entire spectrum of human values becomes vivid. But only a few can find in the Book of books the inspiring canticles (hymns or songs of praise) that are hidden in its pages; these sacred writings are as timely today as they were when they were written thousands of years ago. With this thought in mind I decided to lift them from the Bible and present these songs in a format that would give to today's men and women an insight into the wisdom and treasure they contain. Arranged in a single volume they form an exquisite rendering of supplication and homage to the Lord.

The canticles, like the psalms, are songs or hymns of thanksgiving and praise; they are also devout prayers, and they were principally chanted by ancient Israel to express its gratitude to a merciful and bountiful God. These prayerful canticles are scattered through many books of the Old Testament, including those books which some know as the Apocrypha, and three occur in the New Testament in the Gospel of Luke.

But the canticles are much more than mere hymns and prayers. Through them we can observe the unfolding drama of God's covenant to his people. Through them the reader can witness and relive the primitive history of the people of Israel; he can see them as they suffer persecution, famine, disease, death, and wars; he can journey with God's chosen people from one wilderness to another; he can hear their complaints, witness their tribulations and despair. The reader is moved when he listens to their fervent prayer which begs for the mercy and bounty of God to descend upon them. Reading the inspired canticles gives one a broader perspective of the events that led to the coming of the Messiah.

It is Moses, the great lawgiver, who begins the absorbing narrative of the plight of early man; step by step each song graphically brings into sharp focus the Messiah, who, through the tragic suffering of Israel, comes closer and closer to the fulfillment of his promise to the chosen people, and finally in the Gospel of Saint Luke we share in the joy and beauty with which he was received into the world. And the reader, as he reads on, becomes at once an active participant in the movement of a great prophecy and he remains with its memorable history of growth until the new covenant is brought into being. The hungry soul of man is enriched by sharing in this journey with God and the Israelites.

Come let us spend a moment with God. There is in each canticle the power to illumine those lonely, dark corridors of the mind. As their brilliant light enters the heart we recall those unforgettable words of the late Tom Dooley who wrote to his mother from Hong Kong during his last illness: "I have monstrous phantoms. Inside and outside the wind blows but there are times when the storm around me does not matter. A wilder storm of peace gathers in my heart. What seems unpossessable, I can possess. What seems unfathomable, I can fathom. What is unutterable, I can utter. Because I can pray, I can communicate. How do people endure anything on earth if they cannot have God?"

Surely the demands and pressures of everyday living aren't that urgent that we can't spend a few minutes a day in the company of a God who is always receptive to our pleas and prayers. These stolen moments may, in time, become a part of our daily routine.

How much richer man would be if he knew the ways of God. *Moments with God* is an attempt to present "the background of our Creator and Redeemer." God's revelation of himself in words of wisdom comes to us from the lips of the prophets and as they speak or chant their songs or prayers we see the God of ancient Israel guiding and instructing the chosen people with his boundless love and patience.

Through these sacred hymns we learn that we must, in order to avoid a narrow and confused conception of God, recognize that God took steps to prepare mankind for the appearance of the Messiah, who in the fullness of time would reunite all things in himself. The truth of this is beautifully demonstrated when Christ spoke to the multitude: "Do not think that I have come to do away with the Law of Moses and the teachings of the prophets. I have not come to do away with them, but to make their teachings come true. Remember that as long as heaven and earth last, not the least point nor the smallest detail of the Law will be done away with—not until the end of all things" (Matthew 5:17–18).

But more than that, *Moments with God* is another link in the chain that can bring man closer to God. Saint Augustine's love for the canticles was expressed centuries ago when he cried out: "I wept at the beauty of your hymns and canticles, and was powerfully moved at the sweet sound of your Church's singing. Those sounds flowed into my ears, and the truth streamed into my heart; so that my feeling of devotion overflowed, and the tears ran from my eyes and I was happy in them."

Each canticle is preceded by an explanatory note that highlights the background and setting of the song which should give the reader an insight into the hymn and the purpose behind it.

1

The Song of Moses

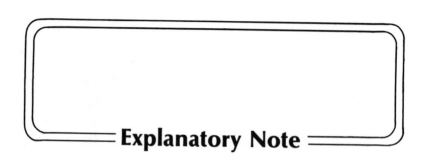

Explanatory Note

After the tenth plague struck the land of Egypt, Pharaoh "sent for Moses and Aaron and said, 'Get out, you and your Israelites! Leave my country; go and worship the Lord, as you asked. Take your sheep, goats, and cattle, and leave. Also pray for a blessing on me' " (Exodus 12:31–32).

And the chosen people, with the angel of God guiding them, made ready to depart. But as the Jews marched in song and triumph, Pharaoh and his servants had a change of heart. Angrily they exclaimed "What have we done? We have let the Israelites excape, and we have lost them as our slaves!" (Exodus 14:5). And immediately Pharaoh and his warriors in six hundred chariots pursued Israel while they marched to their freedom. The people turned and saw the Egyptians on the march; Pharaoh and his huge army were already upon them, and in great fear the Israelites cried out to the God of Israel.

And following the miraculous drowning of the Egyptian forces and the victorious crossing of the Red Sea, the Jews sang this song which Moses had written. It beautifully details the conquest over their persecutors and its consequences. Their hymn of praise, joy, and thanksgiving forcefully demonstrates the intense love which God has for all his children, for he never ceases to do wonderful things for us. We have only to "knock and the door shall open."

The Song of Moses

Exodus 15:1–18

"I will sing to the Lord, because he has won a glorious victory;
  he has thrown the horses and their riders into the sea.
The Lord is my strong defender;
  he is the one who has saved me.
He is my God, and I will praise him,
  my father's God, and I will sing about his greatness.
The Lord is a warrior;
  the Lord is his name.

"He threw Egypt's army and its chariots into the sea;
  the best of its officers were drowned in the Red Sea.
The deep sea covered them;
  they sank to the bottom like a stone.

"Your right hand, Lord, is awesome in power;
  it breaks the enemy in pieces.
In majestic triumph you overthrow your foes;
  your anger blazes out and burns them up like straw.
You blew on the sea and the water piled up high;
  it stood up straight like a wall;
  the deepest part of the sea became solid.
The enemy said, 'I will pursue them and catch them;
  I will divide their wealth and take all I want;
  I will draw my sword and take all they have.'
But one breath from you, Lord, and the Egyptians were drowned;
  they sank like lead in the terrible water.

"Lord, who among the gods is like you?
  Who is like you, wonderful in holiness?
  Who can work miracles and mighty acts like yours?

You stretched out your right hand,
  and the earth swallowed our enemies.
Faithful to your promise, you led the people you had rescued;
  by your strength you guided them to your sacred land.
The nations have heard, and they tremble with fear;
  the Philistines are seized with terror.
The leaders of Edom are terrified;
  Moab's mighty men are trembling;
  the people of Canaan lose their courage.
Terror and dread fall upon them.
They see your strength, O Lord,
  and stand helpless with fear
  until your people have marched past—
  the people you set free from slavery.
You bring them in and plant them on your mountain,
  the place that you, Lord, have chosen for your home,
  the Temple that you yourself have built.
You, Lord, will be king forever and ever."

2

The Song of Moses

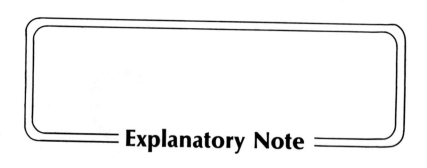

Explanatory Note

As the Israelites were getting closer to the Promised Land, they forgot the bounty and mercy of God. Rather than being grateful for their deliverance from the bondage of the Egyptians, they fell to sin and idol worship. Their ingratitude knew no bounds. And Moses, in a voice tinged with anger, spoke. The words of his song were like searing flames. They reminded the Jews of God's goodness, of his perfect justice, and of God's anger towards a people who were unfaithful. So also today the wrath of God can fall upon those who wander from the fold.

The Song of Moses

Deuteronomy 32:1–43

"Earth and sky, hear my words,
    listen closely to what I say.
My teaching will fall like drops of rain
    and form on the earth like dew.
My words will fall like showers on young plants,
    like gentle rain on tender grass.
I will praise the name of the Lord,
    and his people will tell of his greatness.

"The Lord is your mighty defender,
    perfect and just in all his ways;
Your God is faithful and true;
    he does what is right and fair.
But you are unfaithful, unworthy to be his people,
    a sinful and deceitful nation.
Is this the way you should treat the Lord,
    you foolish, senseless people?
He is your father, your Creator,
    he made you into a nation.

"Think of the past, of the time long ago;
    ask your fathers to tell you what happened,
    ask the old men to tell of the past.
The Most High assigned nations their lands;
    he determined where peoples should live.
He assigned to each nation a heavenly being,
    but Jacob's descendants he chose for himself.

"He found them wandering through the desert,
    a desolate, wind-swept wilderness.

19

He protected them and cared for them,
  as he would protect himself.
Like an eagle teaching its young to fly,
  catching them safely on its spreading wings,
  the Lord kept Israel from falling.
The Lord alone led his people
  without the help of a foreign god.

"He let them rule the highlands,
  and they ate what grew in the fields.
They found wild honey among the rocks;
  their olive trees flourished in stony ground.
Their cows and goats gave plenty of milk;
  they had the best sheep, goats, and cattle,
  the finest wheat, and the choicest wine.

"The Lord's people grew rich, but rebellious;
  they were fat and stuffed with food.
They abandoned God their Creator
  and rejected their mighty savior.
Their idolatry made the Lord jealous;
  the evil they did made him angry.
They sacrificed to gods that are not real,
  new gods their ancestors had never known,
  gods that Israel had never obeyed.
They forgot their god, their mighty savior,
  the one who had given them life.

"When the Lord saw this, he was angry
  and rejected his sons and daughters.
'I will no longer help them,' he said;
  'then I will see what happens to them,
  those stubborn, unfaithful people.
With their idols they have made me angry,
  jealous with their so-called gods,
  gods that are really not gods.
So I will use a so-called nation to make them angry;
  I will make them jealous with a nation of fools.
My anger will flame up like fire
  and burn everything on earth.

It will reach to the world below
    and consume the roots of the mountains.

" 'I will bring on them endless disasters
    and use all my arrows against them.
They will die from hunger and fever;
    they will die from terrible diseases.
I will send wild animals to attack them,
    and poisonous snakes to bite them.
War will bring death in the streets;
    terrors will strike in the homes.
Young men and young women will die;
    neither babies nor old men will be spared.
I would have destroyed them completely,
    so that no one would remember them.
But I could not let their enemies boast
    that they had defeated my people,
    when it was I myself who had crushed them.'

"Israel is a nation without sense;
    they have no wisdom at all.
They fail to see why they were defeated;
    they cannot understand what happened.
Why were a thousand defeated by one,
    and ten thousand by only two?
The Lord, their God, had abandoned them:
    their mighty God had given them up.
Their enemies know that their own gods are weak,
    not mighty like Israel's God.
Their enemies, corrupt as Sodom and Gomorrah,
    are like vines that bear bitter and poisonous grapes,
    like wine made from the venom of snakes.

"The Lord remembers what their enemies have done;
    he waits for the right time to punish them.
The Lord will take revenge and punish them;
    the time will come when they will fall;
    the day of their doom is near.
The Lord will rescue his people

when he sees that their strength is gone.
He will have mercy on those who serve him,
  when he sees how helpless they are.
Then the Lord will ask his people,
  'Where are those mighty gods you trusted?
You fed them with the fat of your sacrifices
  and offered them wine to drink.
Let them come and help you now;
  let them run to your rescue.'

" 'I, and I alone, am God;
  no other god is real.
I kill and I give life, I wound and I heal,
  and no one can oppose what I do.
As surely as I am the living god,
  I raise my hand and I vow
    that I will sharpen my flashing sword
    and see that justice is done.
I will take revenge on my enemies
  and punish those who hate me.
My arrows will drip with their blood,
  and my sword will kill all who oppose me.
I will spare no one who fights against me;
  even the wounded and prisoners will die.'

"Nations, you must praise the Lord's people—
  he punishes all who kill them.
He takes revenge on his enemies
  and forgives the sins of his people."

3

The Song of Deborah and Barak

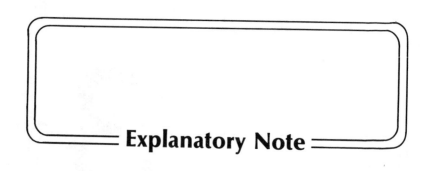

Explanatory Note

The Israelites were forever violating the Law of God and it was during the period of Judges that they fell to worshiping the gods of Baal and Ashtaroth. Their mockery offended God, and "so the Lord became furious with Israel and let raiders attack and rob them. He let enemies all around overpower them, and the Israelites could no longer protect themselves" (Judges 2:14). And as the people toiled and sweated amidst terror and oppression, they cried out to the Lord for deliverance. God, seeing the cruelty and inhumanity inflicted on his children, sent a savior to aid and liberate the people of Israel from their long and arduous servitude under Cushan Rishathaim, king of Mesopotamia.

The freedom of God's people was brought about by Othniel, a savior, and when the spirit of the Lord came to him he defeated the tyrannical king who held the Jews in his power for eight years. And for forty years the people lived by the Law of God and the land was at rest. But when Othniel died, Israel again fell away from God; this time they were crushed and beaten by Eglon, king of Moab. They suffered in his bondage eighteen long years.

Again they pleaded to the God of Israel to shower his mercy upon them. The Lord sent another savior, the Benjaminite Ehud, who brought the Moabites under the power of Israel and they lived in peace, with God and the land, for eighty beautiful and profitable years.

But at the death of Ehud, they quickly drifted away from the Lord's commandments, and the Israelites were now in the power of Jabin, the Canaanite king, who persecuted them cruelly for twenty years with his nine hundred iron chariots. Again the Israelites cried to the Lord for help.

This time their savior was a woman, the judge and prophetess Deborah, who planned her strategy against the king with the cunning of a general. She summoned Barak and said to him: "The

Lord, the God of Israel, has given you this command: 'Take ten thousand men from the tribes of Naphtali and Zebulun and lead them to Mount Tabor. I will bring Sisera, the commander of Jabin's army, to fight you at the Kishon River. He will have his chariots and soldiers, but I will give you victory over him' " (Judges 4:6–7).

But Barak, a little on the weak side, answered: " 'I will go if you go with me, but if you don't go with me, I won't go either.' She answered, 'All right, I will go with you, but you won't get any credit for the victory, because the Lord will hand Sisera over to a woman.' So Deborah set off for Kedesh with Barak" (Judges 4:8–9).

Deborah was a woman who fought valiantly for her beliefs and principles, and together with Barak and a huge army they marched on Mount Tabor where they succeeded in freeing Israel from the tyranny of the cruel king. Israel's freedom was doubly assured when Sisera, the general of Jabin's army, after his entire regiment had been wiped out, fled on foot to the tent of Jahel, the wife of Heber the Kenite, who killed him as he was fast asleep with weariness.

Following the conquest of the Canaanites, Deborah and Barak chanted their hymn of thanksgiving, giving praise to the glory of an ever-merciful God. The canticle is an excellent example of primitive Hebrew poetry, and its vivid imagery becomes at once a stern reminder that, though we are but human and subject to error and sin, the mercy and the bounty of the Lord and the forgiveness of sins will never be denied to those who seek it, no matter how often the heavenly gates are stormed.

The Song of Deborah and Barak

Judges 5:1–31

Praise the Lord!
   The Israelites were determined to fight;
   the people gladly volunteered.
Listen, you kings!
   Pay attention, you rulers!
I will sing and play music
   to Israel's God, the Lord.
Lord, when you left the mountains of Seir,
   when you came out of the region of Edom,
   the earth shook, and rain fell from the sky.
   Yes, water poured down from the clouds.
The mountains quaked before the Lord of Sinai,
   before the Lord, the God of Israel.

In the days of Shamgar son of Anath,
   in the days of Jael,
caravans no longer went through the land,
   and travelers used the back roads.
The towns of Israel stood abandoned, Deborah;
   they stood empty until you came,
   came like a mother for Israel.
Then there was war in the land
   when the Israelites chose new gods.
Of the forty thousand men in Israel,
   did anyone carry shield or spear?
My heart is with the commanders of Israel,
   with the people who gladly volunteered.
   Praise the Lord!

26

Tell of it, you that ride on white donkeys,
  sitting on saddles,
  and you that must walk wherever you go.
Listen! The noisy crowds around the wells
  are telling of the Lord's victories,
  the victories of Israel's people!
Then the Lord's people marched down from their cities.
Lead on, Deborah, lead on!
  Lead on! Sing a song! Lead on!
Forward, Barak son of Abinoam,
  lead your captives away!
Then the faithful ones came down to their leaders;
  the Lord's people came to him ready to fight.
They came from Ephraim into the valley,
  behind the tribe of Benjamin and its people.
The commanders came down from Machir,
  the officers down from Zebulun.
The leaders of Issachar came with Deborah;
  yes, Issachar came and Barak too,
  and they followed him into the valley.
But the tribe of Reuben was divided;
  they could not decide to come.
Why did they stay behind with the sheep?
  To listen to shepherds calling the flocks?
Yes, the tribe of Reuben was divided;
  they could not decide to come.
The tribe of Gad stayed east of the Jordan,
  and the tribe of Dan remained by the ships.
The tribe of Asher stayed by the seacoast;
  they remained along the shore.
But the people of Zebulun and Naphtali
  risked their lives on the battlefield.

At Taanach, by the stream of Megiddo,
  the kings of Canaan fought;
the kings of Canaan fought,
  but they took no silver away.
The stars fought from the sky;
  as they moved across the sky,

they fought against Sisera.
A flood in the Kishon swept them away—
the onrushing Kishon River.
I shall march, march on, with strength!
Then the horses came galloping on,
stamping the ground with their hooves.
"Put a curse on Meroz," says the angel of the Lord,
"a curse, a curse on those who live there.
They did not come to help the Lord,
come as soldiers to fight for him."

The most fortunate of women is Jael,
the wife of Heber the Kenite—
the most fortunate of women who live in tents.
Sisera asked for water, but she gave him milk;
she brought him cream in a beautiful bowl.
She took a tent peg in one hand,
a workman's hammer in the other;
she struck Sisera and crushed his skull;
she pierced him through the head.
He sank to his knees,
fell down and lay still at her feet.
At her feet he sank to his knees and fell;
he fell to the ground, dead.

Sisera's mother looked out of the window;
she gazed from behind the lattice.
"Why is his chariot so late in coming?" she asked.
"Why are his horses so slow to return?"
Her wisest ladies answered her,
and she told herself over and over,
"They are only finding things to capture and divide,
a girl or two for every soldier,
rich cloth for Sisera,
embroidered pieces for the neck of the queen."

So may all your enemies die like that, O Lord,
but may your friends shine like the rising sun!

And there was peace in the land for forty years.

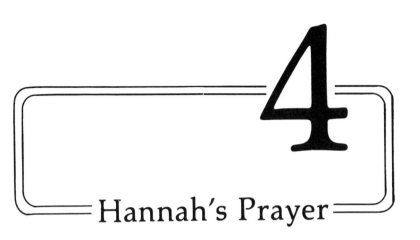

4

Hannah's Prayer

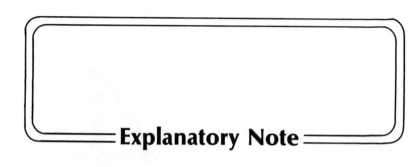

Explanatory Note

Elkanah was married to Hannah who was barren. Hannah knew that her husband would be joyous if she were to be with child. So she prayed to the Lord for a son and, in time, the gift of life was bestowed upon her. Soon after the miraculous conception and birth of her son Samuel, she wrote her song of praise and love, which nobly expresses her strong faith and confidence in the providence of God. The canticle ends with a prophecy about the coming of the Son of God. Hannah's prayer is a continuous reminder that "man is not strong by his own strength."

Hannah's Prayer

1 Samuel 2:1–10

"The Lord has filled my heart with joy;
   how happy I am because of what he has done!
I laugh at my enemies;
   how joyful I am because God has helped me!

"No one is holy like the Lord;
   there is none like him,
   no protector like our God.
Stop your loud boasting;
   silence your proud words.
For the Lord is a God who knows,
   and he judges all that people do.
The bows of strong soldiers are broken,
   but the weak grow strong.
The people who once were well fed
   now hire themselves out to get food,
   but the hungry are hungry no more.
The childless wife has borne seven children,
   but the mother of many is left with none.
The Lord kills and restores to life;
   he sends people to the world of the dead
   and brings them back again.
He makes some men poor and others rich;
   he humbles some and makes others great.
He lifts the poor from the dust
   and raises the needy from their misery.
He makes them companions of princes
   and puts them in places of honor.
The foundations of the earth belong to the Lord;
   on them he has built the world.

"He protects the lives of his faithful people,
  but the wicked disappear in darkness;
  a man does not triumph by his own strength.
The Lord's enemies will be destroyed;
  he will thunder against them from heaven.
The Lord will judge the whole world;
  he will give power to his king,
  he will make his chosen king victorious."

5

The Song of David

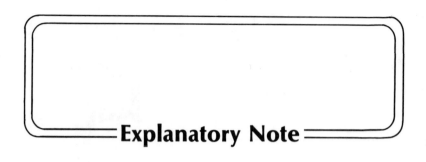

Explanatory Note

The aged King David spent the last days of his life praying and thanking a beneficent and faithful God. The people thronged about him as he praised the Lord. Among other things, David declared that all power comes from God and whatever be the lot of man, worldly accomplishments, fortunes, defeats, and successes, all originate from Almighty God. David's canticle of gratitude and love tells one that everything in heaven and on earth belongs to God and is loaned to us by him, and therefore we should be generous in all things.

The Song of David

1 Chronicles 29:10–13

"Lord God of our ancestor Jacob, may you be praised forever and ever! You are great and powerful, glorious, splendid, and majestic. Everything in heaven and earth is yours, and you are king, supreme ruler over all. All riches and wealth come from you; you rule everything by your strength and power; and you are able to make anyone great and strong. Now, our God, we give you thanks, and we praise your glorious name."

2077874

6

The Song of Tobit

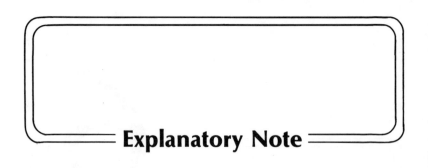

Explanatory Note

Our daily existence is a challenge which sometimes destroys those who possess little faith. Tobias had a tremendous cross to bear. Yet he never permitted himself the folly of listening to the taunts and promises of the devil; he prayed for guidance and strength. In this moving canticle old Tobias gives thanks to God for having sent the archangel Raphael to guide and sustain his family. Through the intercession of the angel, Tobias's eyesight is restored and his young son returns home safely from a dangerous journey. Tobias's words beautifully chant the praises of the power and majesty that is in the spirit and person of God, and this greatness of God can become an integral part of our everyday life if we would but "knock and seek."

The Song of Tobit

Tobit 13:1–9

"Praise the eternal God,
    praise the one who rules.
He punishes us; then he shows us mercy.
    He sends us down to the world of the dead,
    then he brings us up from the grave.
No one can escape his power.

"People of Israel, give thanks among the nations,
    where he sent you into exile;
    even there he showed his great power.
Let all who live hear your praise.
The Lord is our God and father forever.

"Though he punished you for your wickedness,
    he will be merciful and bring you home
    from among the nations where he scattered you.

"Turn to him with all your heart and soul,
    live in loyal obedience to him.
    Then he will turn to you to help you
    and will no longer hide himself.
Remember what God has done for you,
    and give thanks with all your heart.
Praise the righteous Lord;
    honor the eternal King.
"Although I live in exile in a foreign land,
    I will give thanks to the Lord
    and will speak of his great strength to a nation of sinners.
'Turn away from your sins, and do what pleases God!

Perhaps he will be gracious
   and show you his mercy.'

"I praise my God and rejoice in his greatness
   my whole being honors the King of heaven.

"Let everyone tell of his greatness
   and sing his praises in Jerusalem.

"Jerusalem, Holy City of our God,
   he will punish you for the sins of your people,
   but he will be merciful to all who do right."

The Song of Judith

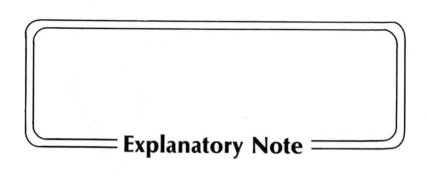

Explanatory Note

The people of Bethulia were virtual prisoners of the Assyrians who were under the command of General Holofernes. "The cisterns of water were going dry, and they did not have enough water to drink their fill for a single day" (Judith 7:21). Faint from thirst and loss of heart, they prayed for deliverance. At this point, Judith appeared on the scene and her faith, valor, and heroic love of country gave the Israelites the courage they needed.

Judith, in a sense, was a soldier of the Lord. She sought ways to free the sieged city. She pleaded with God and soon she knew what had to be done. During the height of the persecution when Holofernes and his soldiers were ready to destroy Israel, Judith quietly journeyed to Holofernes's chambers. He was drunk and deep in sleep. She stood before the bed and said, "Strengthen me, O Lord God of Israel; and in this hour look on the works of my hands" (Judith 13:7). And quickly she took his own sword which hung nearby and cut off the general's head.

In this brief canticle Judith extols her gratitude to Almighty God who had given her the strength to carry out her mighty deed. Her song strongly demonstrates that "With men it is impossible, but not with God; for all things are possible with God."

The Song of Judith

Judith 16:13–17

"I will sing a new song to my God.
    O Lord, you are strong and glorious!
    You have never been defeated.
Let all your creatures serve you.
    You gave the command,
    and all of them came into being;
    you breathed on them,
    and all of them were created.
    No one can oppose your command.
The mountains and the seas tremble,
    and rocks melt like wax when you come near.
But there is mercy for all who obey you.
The Lord is more pleased with those who obey him
    than with all the choice meat on the altar,
    or with all the most fragrant sacrifices.
The nations who rise up against my people are doomed.
    The Lord Almighty will punish them on Judgment Day.
    He will send fire and worms to devour their bodies,
    and they will weep in pain forever."

8

The Song of Ecclesiasticus

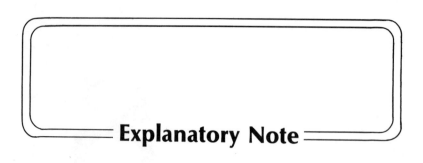

Explanatory Note

The time of Jesus Sirach, the author of this prayerful canticle, was a period of divided kingdoms, oppression, and persecution. Israel kept begging the Lord that he manifest his love and mercy to them by punishing the oppressors of his chosen people, and thus prove to the Israelites that he was the one true, eternal God.

The canticle is a fervent prayer for the scattered tribes of Jacob to unite and worship in one temple. It also renders in telling language a plea to the Almighty that he show his miraculous deeds, as in the past, and reveal his terrible anger to the godless, that they may come to believe in him and live their lives upholding his commandments. But more than that, the poignant words of supplication bring to mind that we should look to Paradise, "for here we have no permanent city, but we seek for the city that is to come."

The Song of Ecclesiasticus

Ecclesiasticus (Sirach) 36:1–17

O Lord God of the universe, look upon us and have mercy. Make every nation stand in fear of you. Take action against the foreign nations, and let them witness your power! You have used us to show them how holy you are; now use them to show us how great you are. Let them learn, as we have learned, that there is no God, O Lord, but you. Give new signs, perform new miracles; show us your glorious strength! Bring on that appointed time when everyone can talk about the great things you do. Pour out your furious, flaming anger, and let none of our enemies survive. Destroy those who have oppressed your people. Crush all those enemy rulers who think they are the only people in the world who matter! Gather the tribes of Israel together again, and give them back their land as you gave it to them long ago. Lord, have mercy on Israel, the people who are known by your name, whom you called your first-born son. Take pity on Jerusalem, your holy city, where you chose to stay. Fill your Temple on Mount Zion with your glory and with hymns of praise. Testify for your people, whom you created in the beginning; fulfill the prophecies that have been spoken in your name. Reward those who have put their faith in you, and vindicate your prophets. You have always been gracious to your people; listen to your servants as we pray. Then everyone on earth will recognize that you are the Lord, the God of the ages.

The Song of Isaiah

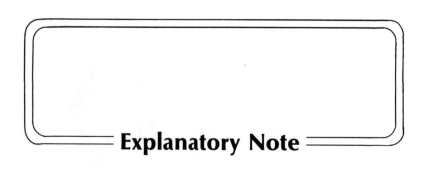

Explanatory Note

The prophet Isaiah had a tremendous passion for the salvation of Israel. His words to the people of Israel had a power which strengthened their confidence in the Messiah who was yet to come. Here he predicts that the chosen people will ultimately praise God, their deliverer from the tyranny of the Assyrians, as their fathers had glorified him after he had given them their freedom from the Egyptians.

The canticle's spirit of hope and love comes forth when Isaiah predicts the glory and majesty that will be with the world at the coming of the Savior of humankind.

The Song of Isaiah

Isaiah 12:1–6

A day is coming when people will sing,
"I praise you, Lord! You were angry with me,
  but now you comfort me and are angry no longer.
God is my savior;
  I will trust him and not be afraid.
The Lord gives me power and strength;
  he is my savior.
As fresh water brings joy to the thirsty,
  so God's people rejoice when he saves them."
A day is coming when people will sing,
"Give thanks to the Lord! Call for him to help you!
  Tell all the nations what he has done!
  Tell them how great he is!
Sing to the Lord because of the great things he has done.
  Let the whole world hear the news.
Let everyone who lives in Zion shout and sing!
  Israel's holy God is great,
    and he lives among his people."

10

The Song of Isaiah

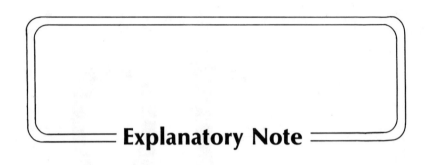

Explanatory Note

The prophet Isaiah was primarily concerned with justice and adherence to the Law of God. He stood like an impenetrable fortress in his mission to conquer idolatry and the social abuses that were rampant in his day.

He strongly attacked the rich and those who were in power; and to the Israelites who fell into profligate and hypocritical ways, his scorn and fiery words were like a whip lashing at their guilt: he exhorted them to repent from their sins and return to the commandments of the Lord before the wrath of God descended upon them.

His was a selfless and dedicated apostleship of prayer and hope. His canticle speaks of the victory and the glory that will be with the universe at the coming of the Messiah.

Isaiah's song of redemptive joy brings to mind these thoughts: Lord, we pray not for tranquillity; we pray that Thou grant us strength and grace to overcome adversity, the chaos, the racial intolerance, and the bigotry that engulf the world today.

The Song of Isaiah

Isaiah 26:1–19

A day is coming when the people will sing this song
  in the land of Judah:
Our city is strong!
God himself defends its walls!
Open the city gates
  and let the faithful nation enter,
  the nation whose people do what is right.
You, Lord, give perfect peace
  to those who keep their purpose firm
  and put their trust in you.
Trust in the Lord forever;
  he will always protect us.
He has humbled those who were proud;
  he destroyed the strong city they lived in,
  and sent its walls crashing into the dust.

Those who were oppressed walk over it now
  and trample it under their feet.
Lord, you make the path smooth for good men;
  the road they travel is level.
We follow your will and put our hope in you;
  you are all that we desire.
At night I long for you with all my heart;
  when you judge the earth and its people,
  they will all learn what justice is.
Even though you are kind to wicked men,
  they never learn to do what is right.
Even here in a land of righteous people they still do wrong;
  they refuse to recognize your greatness.

Your enemies do not know that you will punish them.
Lord, put them to shame and let them suffer;
    let them suffer the punishment you have prepared.
Show them how much you love your people.

You will give us prosperity, Lord;
    everything that we achieve
    is the result of what you do.
Lord our God, we have been ruled by others,
    but you alone are our Lord.
Now they are dead and will not live again;
    their ghosts will not rise,
    for you have punished them and destroyed them.
No one remembers them any more.
Lord, you have made our nation grow,
    enlarging its territory on every side,
    and this has brought you honor.
You punished your people, Lord,
    and in anguish they prayed to you.
You, Lord, have made us cry out,
    as a woman in labor cries out in pain.
We were in pain and agony,
    but we gave birth to nothing.
We have won no victory for our land;
    we have accomplished nothing.

Those of our people who have died will live again!
Their bodies will come back to life.
All those sleeping in their graves
    will wake up and sing for joy.
As the sparkling dew refreshes the earth,
    so the Lord will revive those who have long been dead.

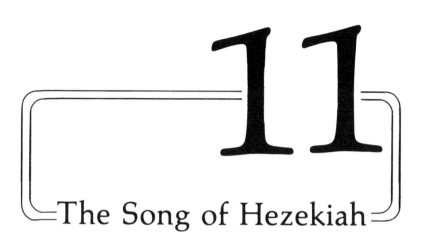

11

The Song of Hezekiah

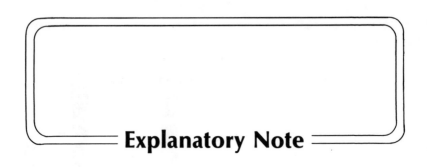

Explanatory Note

When King Hezekiah fell ill, he was visited by Isaiah who said to him, "Put everything in order because you will not recover. Get ready to die." And the dying king turned and stared at the blank wall, his trembling body gripped by fear and sorrow. His soul was clouded with sin, and the torment that had fallen upon him moved the king to tears and prayer.

His prayerful canticle poignantly speaks of his remorse, of his love for the Almighty who had never really deserted him, and of his sincere desire to make his peace with the God of Israel.

Hezekiah was truly penitent. He prayed not for a healthy body, he was primarily interested in forgiveness and the salvation of his soul. The grace of God came to him: he was restored to health and lived a long, fruitful, and godly life.

The Song of Hezekiah

Isaiah 38:10–20

I thought that in the prime of life
I was going to the world of the dead,
Never to live out my life.
I thought that in this world of the living
I would never again see the Lord
Or any living person.
My life was cut off and ended,
Like a tent that is taken down,
Like cloth that is cut from a loom.
I thought that God was ending my life.
All night I cried out with pain,
As if a lion were breaking my bones.
I thought that God was ending my life.
My voice was thin and weak,
And I moaned like a dove.
My eyes grew tired from looking to heaven.
Lord, rescue me from all this trouble.
What can I say? The Lord has done this.
My heart is bitter, and I cannot sleep.

Lord, I will live for you, for you alone;
Heal me and let me live.
My bitterness will turn into peace.
You save my life from all danger;
You forgive all my sins.
No one in the world of the dead can praise you;
The dead cannot trust in your faithfulness.
It is the living who praise you,
As I praise you now.
Fathers tell their children how faithful you are.

Lord, you have healed me.
We will play harps and sing your praise,
Sing praise in your Temple as long as we live.

12

The Song of Isaiah

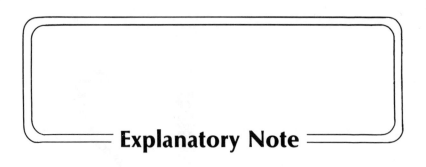

Explanatory Note

Isaiah was a prophet of consolation and hope. To the Israelites he was the light that guided them in the ways of the Lord. His conception of God achieves majestic heights when he speaks of him as the Creator of the Universe and the Savior of man.

The stirring words of this canticle are a convincing argument against those skeptics who refuse to accept or believe in the divine providence of God. Aside from driving home an unshakable premise on the existence of a Supreme Being, he also draws out his prophecy concerning Cyrus, King of Persia, who was to conquer Babylon and allow Israel to return to their native land and later rebuild Jerusalem and the Temple.

Here we see the God of Israel in all his glory. He is the one true God who has remained faithful in his promises to Israel, and Isaiah, who has predicted the restoration of the Jews from exile and who saw their triumphant future, glorifies the Lord whose promise of rescue is not only for Israel, but for people all over the world.

The Song of Isaiah

Isaiah 45:15–25

The God of Israel, who saves his people,
   is a God who conceals himself.
Those who make idols will all be ashamed;
   all of them will be disgraced.
But Israel is saved by the Lord,
   and her victory lasts forever;
   her people will never be disgraced.

The Lord created the heavens—
   he is the one who is God!
He formed and made the earth—
   he made it firm and lasting.
He did not make it a desolate waste,
   but a place for people to live.
It is he who says, "I am the Lord,
   and there is no other god.
I have not spoken in secret
   or kept my purpose hidden.
I did not require the people of Israel
   to look for me in a desolate waste.
I am the Lord, and I speak the truth;
   I make known what is right."

The Lord says,
   "Come together, people of the nations,
   all who survive the fall of the empire;
   present yourselves for the trial!
The people who parade with their idols of wood
   and pray to gods that cannot save them—
   those people know nothing at all!

Come and present your case in court;
   let the defendants consult one another.
Who predicted long ago what would happen?
Was it not I, the Lord, the God who saves his people?
   There is no other god.

"Turn to me now and be saved,
   people all over the world!
I am the only God there is.
My promise is true,
   and it will not be changed.
I solemnly promise by all that I am:
   Everyone will come and kneel before me
   and vow to be loyal to me.

"They will say that only through me
   are victory and strength to be found;
   but all who hate me will suffer disgrace.
I, the Lord, will rescue all the descendants of Jacob,
   and they will give me praise."

13

The Song of Jeremiah

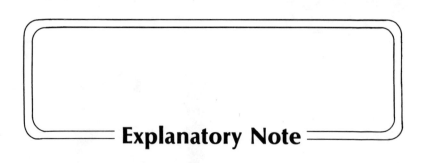

Explanatory Note

Like Isaiah, the prophet Jeremiah fortells the end of the Babylonian exile and describes the gifts and joys that the Lord has in store for his children upon their return to Palestine. And he admonishes the nations openly to confess that the Lord, like a shepherd, is certain to round up his scattered flock and redeem it from its godless persecutors.

And finally, he depicts the joyous, triumphant Israelites marching to the Temple of the Lord on Mount Zion, chanting hymns of praise and thanksgiving.

The canticle reminds us of the good news that Jesus Christ came on earth to save us. He is our shepherd who gathers his scattered children and guards his flock. We have but to seek him.

The Song of Jeremiah

Jeremiah 31:10–14

"Nations, listen to me,
  and proclaim my words on the far-off shores.
I scattered my people, but I will gather them
  and guard them as a shepherd guards his flock.
I have set Israel's people free
  and have saved them from a mighty nation.
They will come and sing for joy on Mount Zion
  and be delighted with my gifts—
  gifts of grain and wine and olive oil,
  gifts of sheep and cattle.
They will be like a well-watered garden;
  they will have everything they need.
Then the girls will dance and be happy,
  and men, young and old, will rejoice.
I will comfort them and turn their mourning into joy,
  their sorrow into gladness.
I will fill the priests with the richest food
  and satisfy all the needs of my people.
I, the Lord, have spoken."

14

The Song of the Three Young Men

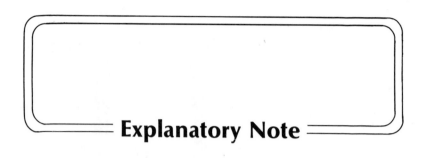

Explanatory Note

King Nebuchadnezzar built a golden statue which he set up in Dura, in the province of Babylon. He then instructed his subjects to prostrate themselves at the altar of the idol and worship it, and whoever did not obey his command would immediately be thrown into a white-hot furnace.

In the king's service were three young, brilliant administrators who ignored the royal command and openly refused to worship a false god. The king became furious and ordered his servants to bind the disloyal youths and cast them into the furnace; and as the iron door of the furnace was jammed shut and the fire blazed, the men inside, whose hearts were imbued with the spirit of the God of Israel, began walking about in the flames, singing and blessing the Lord with their canticle of love and praise.

And when Shadrach, Meshach, and Abednego came out of the furnace, the astonished king proclaimed: "Blessed be the God of these men who sent his angel to deliver the servants that trusted in him; they disobeyed the royal command and yielded their bodies rather than serve or worship any god except their own God."

The canticle of the three Hebrew youths who were saved from a fiery death is emphatic in its message which tells us that in time of distress we should turn our hearts toward God who in his mercy will aid and comfort the soul.

The Song of the Three Young Men

Daniel 3:29–68

"We praise you, O Lord, the God of our ancestors,
May your glorious, holy name
  be held in honor and reverence forever.
May hymns be sung to your glory forever
  and may your holy presence be praised in that temple,
  where you sit on your heavenly throne above
    the winged creatures
  and look down to the world of the dead.
  May you be praised and honored forever.
May you be praised as you sit on your royal throne.
  May hymns be sung to your glory forever.

May you be praised in the dome of the heavens.
  May hymns be sung to your glory forever.

"Praise the Lord, all creation;
  sing his praise and honor him forever.
Praise the Lord, skies above;
  sing his praise and honor him forever.
Praise the Lord, all angels of the Lord;
  sing his praise and honor him forever.
Praise the Lord, all waters above the sky;
  sing his praise and honor him forever.
Praise the Lord, all heavenly powers;
  sing his praise and honor him forever.
Praise the Lord, sun and moon;
  sing his praise and honor him forever.
Praise the Lord, stars of heaven;
  sing his praise and honor him forever.
Praise the Lord, rain and dew;
  sing his praise and honor him forever.

71

Praise the Lord, all winds;
  sing his praise and honor him forever.
Praise the Lord, fire and heat;
  sing his praise and honor him forever.
Praise the Lord, bitter cold and scorching heat;
  sing his praise and honor him forever.
Praise the Lord, dews and snows;
  sing his praise and honor him forever.
Praise the Lord, nights and days;
  sing his praise and honor him forever.
Praise the Lord, daylight and darkness;
  sing his praise and honor him forever.
Praise the Lord, ice and cold;
  sing his praise and honor him forever.
Praise the Lord, frost and snow;
  sing his praise and honor him forever.
Praise the Lord, lightning and storm clouds;
  sing his praise and honor him forever.

"Let the earth praise the Lord;
  sing his praise and honor him forever.
Praise the Lord, mountains and hills;
  sing his praise and honor him forever.
Praise the Lord, everything that grows;
  sing his praise and honor him forever.
Praise the Lord, lakes and rivers;
  sing his praise and honor him forever.
Praise the Lord, springs of water;
  sing his praise and honor him forever.
Praise the Lord, whales and sea creatures;
  sing his praise and honor him forever.
Praise the Lord, all birds;
  sing his praise and honor him forever.
Praise the Lord, all cattle and wild animals;
  sing his praise and honor him forever.

"Praise the Lord, all people on earth;
  sing his praise and honor him forever.
Praise the Lord, people of Israel;
  sing his praise and honor him forever.

Praise the Lord, priests of the Lord;
  sing his praise and honor him forever.
Praise the Lord, servants of the Lord;
  sing his praise and honor him forever.
Praise the Lord, all faithful people;
  sing his praise and honor him forever.
Praise the Lord, all who are humble and holy;
  sing his praise and honor him forever.
Praise the Lord, Hananiah, Azariah, and Mishael;
  sing his praise and honor him forever.
He rescued us from the world of the dead
  and saved us from the power of death.
He brought us out from the burning furnace
  and saved us from the fire.
Give thanks to the Lord, for he is good
  and his mercy lasts forever.
Praise the Lord, all who worship him;
  sing praise to the God of gods and give him thanks,
  for his mercy lasts forever."

Jonah's Prayer

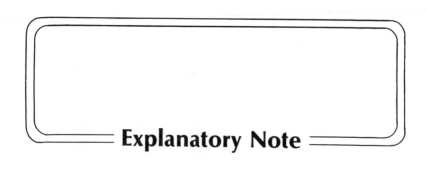

Explanatory Note

The prophet Jonah was a messenger and an early apostle of the God of Israel. One day the word of the Lord came to him: "Go to Nineveh, that great city," said the Lord, "and speak out against it; I am aware of how wicked its people are."

As Jonah pondered the words, he could not grasp why God should be concerned about those heathen so many miles away; actually, Jonah did not care enough to make the journey. The Ninevites were strangers to him and therefore their salvation was not his concern.

So instead of obeying the command of the Lord, stubborn, temperamental Jonah traveled to Joppa where he boarded a vessel that was bound for Spain. He firmly believed that the ship would take him away from the responsibility which God had given him. But God sent a violent storm upon the sea which put the boat in great danger; and Jonah, in the hold of the ship, slept like a baby while the craft was on the point of breaking up.

The frightened crew prayed to their gods and the captain went below and said to Jonah: "What are you doing asleep? Get up and pray to your God for help. Maybe he will feel sorry for us and spare our lives."

Then the fearful sailors spoke among themselves: "Let's draw lots to find out who is to blame for getting us into this danger." And having done so, they singled out the sleepy, bewildered Jonah and said: "Now then, tell us! Who is to blame for this? What are you doing here? What country do you come from?" And Jonah said to them: "I am a Hebrew. I worship the Lord, the God of heaven, who made land and sea." Then he "went on to tell them that he was running away from the Lord."

And they said to him: "That was an awful thing to do! What should we do to stop the storm?"

The spirit of God came to Jonah as he said to the crew: "Throw me into the sea, and it will calm down. I know it is my fault that you are caught in this violent storm," he explained, and the mariners threw him into the sea and immediately the turbulent waters became calm, but Jonah was swallowed by a whale and he remained in the belly of the fish three days and three nights.

Then Jonah began to pray. He begged forgiveness and deliverance. In his canticle there is a fervent plea that his prayer be heard by the Lord whom he had disobeyed. Soon the mercy of God fell upon him and the whale cast him out on a dry beach. And again the voice of the Lord came to Jonah, but this time the prophet sped to Nineveh and like a town crier he roamed the streets announcing: "In forty days Nineveh will be destroyed."

Jonah was amazed that the entire city, from the king down, listened to his message of doom and repented from their sins. They promised to live by the commandments of the Lord and when God saw the sincerity and willingness of the Ninevites he did not fulfill his evil promise to destroy the great city. But the conversion of Nineveh made Jonah angry and the Lord asked him: "What right do you have to be angry?"

Jonah did not reply. In his bitterness he sat outside the city limits to see what would happen to Nineveh; and because God loved him, he provided a plant to protect his head, but in the morning God sent a worm which destroyed the plant. The rising sun began baking the prophet's head until he was almost faint, and in his despair he cried out: "I am better off dead than alive."

And God said to him: "What right do you have to be angry about the plant?"

"I have every right to be angry," the prophet answered, "angry enough to die." And the Lord said to him: "This plant grew up in one day and disappeared the next; you didn't do anything for it and you didn't make it grow—yet you feel sorry for it! How much more, then, should I have pity on Nineveh, that great city. After all it has more than 120,000 innocent children in it, as well as many animals."

And in the New Testament we find Jesus saying in Matthew 12:41-42: "In the same way that Jonah spent three days and three nights in the big fish, so will the Son of Man spend three days and three nights in the depths of the earth. On the Judgment Day the people of Nineveh will stand up and accuse you, because they turned from their sins when they heard Jonah preach; and I tell you that there is something here greater than Jonah!"

The prayerful canticle of Jonah tells us that we can never be entirely free of responsibilities, whether spiritual or worldly. No matter where Jonah traveled, the power and majesty of the Lord was always present. We should never question the wisdom of God, nor run from his grace when it comes to us. Rather we must try to recognize "in him the strength that we ourselves lack."

Jonah's Prayer

Jonah 2:2–10; 4:2–3

"In my distress, O Lord, I called to you,
  and you answered me.
From deep in the world of the dead
  I cried for help, and you heard me.
You threw me down into the depths,
    to the very bottom of the sea,
    where the waters were all around me,
    and all your mighty waves rolled over me.
I thought I had been banished from your presence
    and would never see your holy Temple again.
The water came over me and choked me;
    the sea covered me completely,
    and seaweed wrapped around my head.
I went down to the very roots of the mountains,
    into the land whose gates lock shut forever.
But you, O Lord my God,
    brought me back from the depths alive.
When I felt my life slipping away,
    then, O Lord, I prayed to you,
    and in your holy Temple you heard me.
Those who worship worthless idols
    have abandoned their loyalty to you.
But I will sing praises to you;
    I will offer you a sacrifice
    and do what I have promised.
Salvation comes from the Lord!"

16

Habakkuk's Prayer

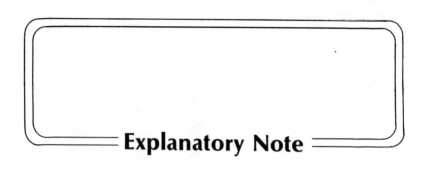

Explanatory Note

It was during the first invasion of Judah by Nebuchadnezzar that the prophet Habakkuk appeared. He fought to bring the fear of God to the people of Israel; the time was ripe for sin and idolatry. The small kingdom was rampant with violence and political intrigue and the spirit of the Lord was not in the hearts of the people.

Then Israel, frightened and bewildered, listened to their courageous prophet who spoke of God's judgments against the wicked; and as he warned them of the Lord's punishment, he also predicted the blessings and rewards to be showered on the just and the faithful by God.

His description of the Almighty coming in judgment is unforgettable. Habakkuk sees God quietly descending to earth as the heavens go into hiding behind the brilliance of his splendor. His arrival brings pestilence, fever, earthquake. The physical world is in a violent storm at his Last Judgment; the sun and moon fade into oblivion as God flashes his weapons of vengeance. In an instant the enemies of Israel are crushed, including their power to rule and conquer.

Terrified at the vision of the judgment, Habakkuk pleads with God to temper his anger with mercy. But he becomes calm and joyous when he remembers that the Judge is the Savior and the courage of Israel.

The canticle is a firm reminder that God gives us crosses to bear and we must never waver or lose faith, for "with faith, there is a prospect that events and experiences will become meaningful; without some faith all experience and all life are meaningless."

Habakkuk's Prayer

Habakkuk 3:2–19

O Lord, I have heard of what you have done,
   and I am filled with awe.
Now do again in our times
   the great deeds you used to do.
Be merciful, even when you are angry.

God is coming again from Edom;
   the holy God is coming from the hills of Paran.
His splendor covers the heavens;
   and the earth is full of his praise.
He comes with the brightness of lightning;
   light flashes from his hand,
   there where his power is hidden.
He sends disease before him
   and commands death to follow him.
When he stops, the earth shakes;
   at his glance the nations tremble.
The eternal mountains are shattered;
   the everlasting hills sink down,
   the hills where he walked in ancient times.

I saw the people of Cushan afraid
   and the people of Midian tremble.
Was it the rivers that made you angry, Lord?
Was it the sea that made you furious?
You rode upon the clouds;
   the storm cloud was your chariot,
   as you brought victory to your people.
You got ready to use your bow,
   ready to shoot your arrows.

Your lightning split open the earth.
When the mountains saw you, they trembled;
　water poured down from the skies.
The waters under the earth roared,
　and their waves rose high.
At the flash of your speeding arrows
　and the gleam of your shining spear,
　the sun and the moon stood still.
You marched across the earth in anger;
　in fury you trampled the nations.
You went out to save your people,
　to save your chosen king.
You struck down the leader of the wicked
　and completely destroyed his followers.
Your arrows pierced the commander of his army
　when it came like a storm to scatter us,
　gloating like those who secretly oppress the poor.
You trampled the sea with your horses,
　and the mighty waters foamed.

I hear all this, and I tremble;
　and my lips quiver with fear.
My body goes limp,
　and my feet stumble beneath me.

I will quietly wait for the time to come
　when God will punish those who attack us.
Even though the fig trees have no fruit
　and no grapes grow on the vines,
even though the olive crop fails
　and the fields produce no grain,
even though the sheep all die
　and the cattle stalls are empty,
I will still be joyful and glad,
　because the Lord God is my savior.
The Sovereign Lord gives me strength.
　He makes me sure-footed as a deer,
　and keeps me safe on the mountains.

17

The Song of Zechariah

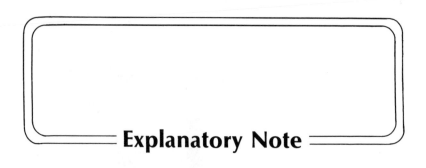

Explanatory Note

During the reign of Herod, king of Judea, there was a priest named Zechariah who was wed to Elizabeth. They upheld the commandments and ordinances of the Lord but their life together would have been richer if they had had children. However, Elizabeth was barren and both were getting on in years.

And as Zechariah was performing his priestly service in the Temple of the Lord, an angel appeared near the altar where incense burned and said: "Don't be afraid, Zechariah! God has heard your prayer, and your wife Elizabeth will bear you a son. You are to name him John. How glad and happy you will be, and how happy many others will be when he is born! He will be a great man in the Lord's sight. He must not drink any wine or strong drink. From his very birth he will be filled with the Holy Spirit, and he will bring back many of the people of Israel to the Lord their God. He will go ahead of the Lord, strong and mighty like the prophet Elijah. He will bring fathers and children together again; he will turn disobedient people back to the way of thinking of the righteous; he will get the Lord's people ready for him" (Luke 1:13–17). Zechariah, doubting the angel, said, "How shall I know if this is so? I am an old man and my wife is old also." And for his lack of faith in believing the words of Gabriel he lost his voice.

And the time came for Elizabeth to have her baby and she gave birth to a son. Her family, together with their friends, rejoiced and praised the Lord for the precious gift. On the eighth day the child was made ready for the ritual of circumcision and the son was to be called Zechariah after his father; but Elizabeth said, "No, his name is to be John."

Finally they made signs to Zechariah and he asked for a slate and on it he wrote the words, "His name is John." And the people were astonished at the agreement of the aged couple and their amazement was beyond them when Zechariah stood up and burst into speech for the first time since the visitation of the angel Gabriel.

In majestic phrases Zechariah, filled with the Spirit, speaks of God's plan for John, a man who was to pave the way, by preaching and baptizing, for the coming of the promised Messiah. John (the Baptist) was the one who baptized the Son of God in the Jordan River.

The canticle recalls the promise of a Redeemer made by God to Abraham. Zechariah's words tell us that God has not forgotten his children and that the day of salvation is at hand: he will free his chosen people so they may serve him without fear and increase in holiness and righteousness before him until the end of time.

In The Benedictus, as this song of praise is known, we learn that Jesus came into the world primarily to save humankind from sin and, therefore, a strong faith, prayer, and adherence to his will should be a part of our everyday living. "To falter in faith or obedience," as the psalmist says, "is to be in darkness and our feet are directed from that inner peace which comes only with faith and obedience."

Let us, with Zechariah, give praise to God for our redemption.

The Song of Zechariah

Luke 1:68–79

"Let us praise the Lord, the God of Israel!
  He has come to the help of his people and has set them free.
He has provided for us a mighty Savior,
  a descendant of his servant David.
He promised through his holy prophets long ago
  that he would save us from our enemies,
  from the power of all those who hate us.
He said he would show mercy to our ancestors
  and remember his sacred covenant.
  With a solemn oath to our ancestor Abraham
  he promised to rescue us from our enemies
  and allow us to serve him without fear,
so that we might be holy and righteous before him
  all the days of our life.

"You, my child, will be called a prophet of the Most High God.
You will go ahead of the Lord
  to prepare his road for him,
to tell his people that they will be saved
  by having their sins forgiven.
Our God is merciful and tender.
He will cause the bright dawn of salvation to rise on us
  and to shine from heaven on all those who live in the dark shadow
    of death,
  to guide our steps into the path of peace."

This song is also known as The Benedictus.

18

Mary's Song of Praise

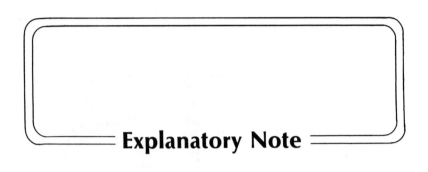

Explanatory Note

We have seen the Israelites live through centuries of war, famine, disease, persecution, and wanderings in the desert. But the protective arm of God and the inspired counsel of the prophets were ever-present to guide and sustain them. And now the Old Law was to be enriched by the New Covenant, which was first announced when the angel Gabriel made his way to a village of Galilee called Nazareth, thus fulfilling God's eternal promise to Abraham to show mercy to Israel.

The special messenger of the "glad tidings" was Gabriel, sent by God to visit the woman who was to be the mother of our Lord. The angel stopped at a poor, humble dwelling of a virgin, betrothed to Joseph and whose name was Mary. As the angel stood before her, he said, "Peace be with you! The Lord is with you and has greatly blessed you!"

Mary was troubled by the angel's message and wondered what the words meant. And again the angel spoke: "Don't be afraid, Mary; God has been gracious to you. You will become pregnant and give birth to a son, and you will name him Jesus. He will be great and will be called the Son of the Most High God . . . his kingdom will never end."

And Mary said, "I am a virgin. How, then, can this be?"

The angel answered: "The Holy Spirit will come on you and God's power will rest upon you. For this reason the holy child will be called the Son of God" (Luke 1:30–35).

And the mother of our Redeemer said: "I am the Lord's servant, may it happen to me as you have said." And the angel left.

Then Mary, her heart a surging river of love and joy, journeys to Judea and when her cousin Elizabeth greets her as the mother of the

Messiah, she responds with a joyful song in which she praises God for the blessing he has bestowed upon her.

This hymn, which is known as The Magnificat, captures the full potency of the graces of God at work: here was an unknown woman of humble origin who lived a quiet existence until the Almighty selected her to become the mother of Jesus, our Lord and Savior.

But what is more, the canticle also makes one think of Mary as a great disciple who spreads God's word and love to the four corners of the earth, for she first gave Christ to the world and thus achieved the essential aim of apostleship.

What a beautiful gift to our Savior if, with Mary as example, we could establish a worldwide chain of lay apostles, an apostolate which could lessen the tensions that beset the world today.

Mary's Song of Praise

Luke 1:46–55

"My heart praises the Lord;
   my soul is glad because of God my Savior,
   for he has remembered me, his lowly servant!
From now on all people will call me happy,
   because of the great things the Mighty God has done for me.
His name is holy;
   from one generation to another
   he shows mercy to those who honor him.
He has stretched out his mighty arm
   and scattered the proud with all their plans.
He has brought down mighty kings from their thrones,
   and lifted up the lowly.
He has filled the hungry with good things,
   and sent the rich away with empty hands.
He has kept the promise he made to our ancestors,
   and has come to the help of his servant Israel.
He has remembered to show mercy to Abraham
   and to all his descendants forever!"

This song is also known as The Magnificat.

19

Simeon's Song

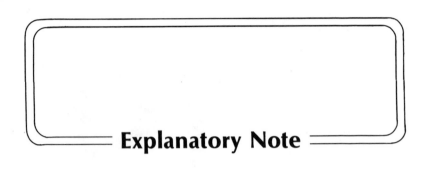

Explanatory Note

Eight days after his birth, when the time came for the baby to be circumcised, Joseph and Mary took Jesus to Jerusalem to present him to the Lord.

In Jerusalem at this time there was a man named Simeon, a righteous and devout soul who was told by the Holy Spirit that he should not see death until he had seen the Lord's promised Messiah. And as the proud, happy parents entered the Temple to fulfill the Law, the pious Simeon, led by the Spirit, walked into the house of the Lord and stood alongside Mary and Joseph as they held the child in their arms.

In an act of love Simeon embraced the Infant Jesus and stared fondly into the eyes of the Son of God. He saw in them the means of salvation, the redemption of the world as God had promised his chosen people through the prophets in the Old Testament.

Now that the aged Simeon had seen the Messiah with his own eyes and fondled him in his own arms, his heart sang out his praises of love and thanksgiving in this four-verse canticle which is known as The Nunc Dimittis. And as the holy family heard his words they marveled at the things Simeon was saying about their son. Then the kindly old man blessed the bewildered parents and to the Mother of the Savior he said: "This child is chosen by God for the destruction and the salvation of many in Israel. He will be a sign from God which many people will speak against and so reveal their secret thoughts." And when Mary and Joseph had fulfilled the Law, they returned to Galilee.

Simeon had a strong and enduring faith and his love for God was a continuous prayer that could be phrased, "O Lord, let us not live to be useless."

Simeon's Song

Luke 2:29–32

"Now, Lord, you have kept your promise,
   and you may let your servant go in peace.
With my own eyes I have seen your salvation,
   which you have prepared in the presence of all peoples:
A light to reveal your will to the Gentiles
   and bring glory to your people Israel."

This song is also known as The Nunc Dimittis.